CHURCH, AGAIN

AGAIN

A Millennial's Desire

NOLAN SOLDAHL

CHURCH, AGAIN

AGAIN

A Millennial's Desire

NOLAN SOLDAHL

Church, Again: A Millennial's Desire
Copyright © 2020 by Nolan Soldahl

ISBN 978-1-7320246-6-3
eISBN 978-1-7320246-7-0

First Edition 2020
10 9 8 7 6 5 4 3 2 1

Printed in the United States of America

Dovestar Publishing International
7149 SC-11, Box 42
Sunset sc, 29685

Cover Photo by <u>Dragos Gontariu</u> on <u>Unsplash</u>

I write this for all those who have shaped my journey so far because they are the reason I have come to love the Church. To my wife, Amber: I know you and I don't always see the same side of the coin, but it is you that grounds me, challenges me, and gives me balance. I will forever choose to treat you as Christ does His Church.

CONTENTS

PROLOGUE

It is my displeasure to know that I am not the only Jesus follower who has felt that church can feel like a prison. On one hand, I know that others have felt the same thing I feel, and it has given me validation (I do not know anyone that doesn't enjoy feeling validated). On the other hand, I am thoroughly saddened that church has felt as if one could not move as God has desired. In writing this, my aim is not to tear down, criticize, or hurt specific local ministries, churches, or even denominations. Rather, I find myself writing from a place of love and concern for the church (as in those who believe in Jesus across the world and create a single "body" of believers).

As I live in the western United States, I am asking this question from a millennial perspective, is the way Church is structured truly the way that it is meant to be? My hope is to encourage leaders to stay humble, be transparent, and empower those they serve with their gifts. May this book only be used to illuminate the Scriptures that have been preserved for us as the Bible. The last thing I want is for this to be used wrongly by a jaded person in a local ministry to confront leadership in a negative way. The Church is not designed to quit on one another but to uphold and admonish without separation, much as Christ does with us.

CHAPTER 1

A MILLENNIAL UNDERSTANDING

❖

"Perceptions may be valid, but not accurate."

Understanding the mindset of the culture I grew up in, including my own, has not been an easy task. The philosophy behind deeds and views today for my generation are unlike any before due to the vast amount of communication and information. I recognize that I am probably the last generation to recall VCR players and a time without smartphones acting as a second brain.

Recently, I looked up on the internet a clear way to distinguish between a millennial and generation "Y." What I found were unconfirmed and conflicting answers. However, most agreed that 1995 was the last year for the millennial while some said '96. Either way, the best answer I have heard and agree with as one caught on the proverbial border is if you were born in the 90's, and your first phone was a smartphone, then you are Gen Y.

This is important because it symbolizes to the millennial a status of having to still memorize things in school, learn cursive, long-hand division, rewind tapes, have CD players that attach to the hip and don't skip or scratch discs, and most importantly not have Bluetooth or Wi-Fi readily available in every home. The point is millennials have had to learn, adapt, and grow with technology and understands the benefits and fruits of the tech industry.

As this happened, many of us grew up with the ability to communicate more and more wide spread than ever before as a natural talent and part of life as opposed to having to learn how to do it over phones that were the size of bricks or attached to landlines. Email revolutionized the ability to send instant messages, Myspace gave one the ability to put their thoughts out there quickly and without care, and talking to someone (or anyone who might care) became a way to care for or ignore a human without ever having to see their face.

This is the environment that the most social and lonely generation had to learn how to navigate. I say that we may be social and active in learning about what one another posts on Facebook, Instagram, or sends us directly through any number of ways, but the human desire is for connection. I know many in my generation who would agree with me when I say that we are connected on a superficial level that does not breed intimacy, trust, and honesty with one another. I take this thought a step further and say that it actually does the opposite by showing only what one wants others to see. When we only show what we want others to see we never truly give them a chance to respond empathetically to the pains of our souls.

Over time and usage of social media we have in fact made ourselves and others more jaded when one shares their deep honest hurts that create vulnerability. I have seen many posts with people who share deep pains and get responses of disbelief or thinking that the person may only be seeking attention. In our attempts to be social, we have become more isolated by our online "communities" than ever. We are designed to seek relationships that are meaningful, and when attempting to capitalize on the technology that is supposed to help us, we fail ourselves as a society and become lonely.

I know that this is not in every specific case scenario. As there are posts of pain with negative responses, I have also seen the opposite happen in social communities online as well. A human struggling with suicidal thoughts may go there to see if anyone really cares or to know if they have made an impact in another's life. On occasion, when this occurs, it is often met with people who recognize distress and are willing to meet the need of the person in pain. This should happen more frequently, but with every Instagram model that posts a photoshopped selfie and Twitter guru that says they dislike something, the negative will always be pointed out and latched onto more than the good.

In the news we always hear what is wrong in the community. Social media often amplifies this sentiment. It is the negative that grabs the attention. From the negative, communities are divided. The good things in our communities get put on standby. I discuss this because it is what feeds our way of thought and comes from the philosophical view of the millennial and generations after.

On the flip side of all that I have said so far, it is far more important that with social media has come a much faster way of getting information out. This includes positive and negative things. The fact that I have seen more positive causes for awareness and people who desire to help the world be a better place with online funding and support is astounding, more so than whatever could be done before!

My concern is this: whatever we see on social media and anywhere else, we can no longer trust and need to vet for facts. If we do not, we face the same issue that Paul did with the early church. Paul wrote letters back to local ministries he helped plant because they had started living wrongly due to misinformation.

> *"I am astonished that you are so quickly deserting him who called you in the grace of Christ and are turning to a different gospel— not that there is another one, but there are some who trouble you and want to distort the gospel of Christ. But even if we or an angel from heaven should preach to you a gospel contrary to the*

one we preached to you, let him be accursed. As we have said before, so now I say again: If anyone is preaching to you a gospel contrary to the one you received, let him be accursed. For am I now seeking the approval of man, or of God? Or am I trying to please man? If I were still trying to please man, I would not be a servant of Christ." Galatians 1:6-10 ESV

In passages like the one above, notice how he opens his letter with how surprised he is that they are believing that which is false. We do this all too often in our understanding of what we see on the internet. What is worse is how we often pick and choose what to believe (not like any of us reading this are guilty of that, especially when it comes to the Bible). With mass communication comes mass lies, truths, and ignorance.

These issues of growing up as a millennial and having to learn how to navigate these webs is why my generation is the way it is and the culture today is what it is. There is no trust in anything except that which one knows to be true: *feelings.*

I believe that emotions may give us a glimpse of honesty into ourselves. This does not mean that we can trust them or that they lead to a correct understanding of an external situation. It does mean that we can learn from them about ourselves. For example, anger gets a bad rap. However, anger is not a bad emotion; it can tell us base truths. One can be angry for many reasons (there is only one acceptable one, injustice according to God's definition of just). When we feel we must ask, "Why do I feel this way about this situation?" This is the beginning of wanting to create an accurate perception of reality.

❖

The heart of the matter is this, perceptions may be valid but not accurate. I have learned to say this a lot in more recent days because the current culture always wants and desires validation for how they feel. Feelings are often what dictate people, and if they are not recognized as valid, it becomes a personal assault on their character which is why others seem to get offended so easily these days.

No matter what one believes anymore, there is only one thing people want you to know, how they feel about something. The base inherent feeling that cannot be argued with is the only way a perception can be valid. This is where perception or view comes in. It is not so much overall objective truth that governs understanding. The emotion that happens in a moment of time for an event that creates a memory is how a person's perception becomes valid. As feelings cannot be argued with, the validity of them and the perception made becomes only their own. Perhaps a better word for valid might be credible.

Once a perception is valid or credible, the person wants it validated. This is dangerous. For a perception to be validated all one needs is to be told that it is accurate by an external trusted source (a person, internet article, bible verse out of context, etc.). This yields to a high probability of that perception being validated within seconds of a Google search. Once validated, its accuracy and entrenchment as a belief may be near impossible to reverse.

I hope by now you understand the gravity of what has been written so far. Due to mass amounts of communication within seconds, perceptions for millennials have been created and validated near instantaneously from birth with little chance for correction. No one knows who to trust. So inevitably, they trust their now validated perceptions that may not be accurate. This is the danger of the millennial point of view, and it is only digressing because people are no longer allowing themselves to be corrected but only validated.

I start this book here as a warning and an alarm so that you may begin to understand why the culture has shaped into what it has. Spiritually speaking, not being able to trust and only be validated through potentially inaccurate perceptions is the ultimate lack of correction in one's life.

Maybe you have already considered all this before, but it is my desire that as followers of Jesus we understand this so that we can love and share the gospel with others in ways they understand. If we continue to allow ourselves to be frustrated with this new adopted mindset by the culture, so much so that we cannot communicate effectively with compassion, then we are only giving the Church a worse cultural image than the one commissioned us by Jesus:

> *"A new commandment I give to you, that you love one another: just as I have loved you, you also are to love one another."* John 13:34 ESV

As a millennial myself, I want you to be reminded that I have had to adopt an outsider perspective while keeping a pulse on understanding my peers. It is not my culture and their ways of thought that rule me any longer, but Jesus and the words preserved for us as Scripture. John 13:34 was from Jesus to His disciples, for disciples, and it continues today for anyone that holds that identity as a disciple of Him.

Jesus makes us all an outsider of our base culture as He calls us into His own: His Church.

CHAPTER 2

PHILOSOPHY

❖

"I'd rather talk philosophy, than discuss Jesus."

When I was in university I was bombarded with critical thinking by a dear friend of mine and several professors. It was a collaborated effort of sabotage to my millennial mind. Even though I had already accepted Jesus into my life and allowed myself to be molded by Him for a couple years prior, it did not change how I thought about reality. Because I am a millennial, I have had tremendous issues garnering a biblical view of the reality that God has created and that my thoughts and beliefs do not change the reality in which I live.

I often use the metaphor of a train. The locomotive will continue on the tracks of life, and you get the chance to jump on or not. This is the same with God and His sovereignty. He will do His will and His plan, and you get the chance to jump on board or watch it roll on by. This metaphor works with the reality. If I believe a blue cup is a red cup and redefine the color blue with red, it will not change the fact that there are measurable wavelengths of light absorbed by the cup making it the frequency that we know to be the color blue.

We are designed to know that there is one reality in which we have one chance to know the One who created it and be the best humans we can be (Ecc. 3:11). The current culture and time in which I write this concerns me because total Truth will not be accepted unless the group one identifies with as part of a validated perception does as well. When I say total Truth with a capital "T," I mean that it is a fact that cannot be changed no matter one's perception or belief about it in accordance with reality.

This needs to be known because it is not only a millennial trait to believe about the world this way but has recently resurfaced as a popular philosophical world view (along with more socialistic tendencies as they go hand in hand). Some of the most popular philosophers of this world view are Immanuel Kant (1972-1804) and Jacques Derrida (1930-2004). Both great thinkers and minds, however, their view of reality is one that is subject to the use of language about it. Think red cup vs scientific fact wavelengths creating a blue cup. The world cannot be what you deem it to simply by saying it is your will.

If one calls themselves a Jesus follower, they cannot honestly hold the view of relativistic postmodernism [1] (a philosophical saying that what one believes about the world actually changes reality). Here is the simple logic train that I needed to kick me in the metaphorical pants in university; if one believes in the God of the Bible, then they must believe that He created everything (the how is not really important) (Gen. 1, Job 37-42). If He created everything, and He is real, then what He created is real outside of what you believe about it.

There is a beauty in this. It leads one to recognize that what He has created is subject to His sovereign will and design (read that Job section, Rom 1:20). In His creation there are ways to analyze and discover facts about what has been created (i.e. atoms, gravity, heat transference). The only thing that is not going to change to His will unless you desire it is you and any other being He gave free will.

When one understands that He made them with free will, and yet is still sovereign and in control of all creation including the spiritual realm, there is a sense of gratitude. If you would like to know more of my personal philosophical views, at the end of this book will be a full essay in which I explain through an illustration of a diver exploring a sunken ship wreck.

❖

Now that a base understanding of philosophy has been discussed, I hope the importance of why one believes this about reality as a Jesus follower is absolutely necessary. If we don't take Paul's words in Romans 1 about creation seriously, it will cause not only creation, but the person of Jesus to lack worth (Rom. 1 20-23). This is the reason that I would rather talk philosophical views of the world with someone before I talk about the ultimate Truth that is Jesus.

The parable of the seed falling on different soil comes to mind. If the person is already rocky soil, I know the seed will not take. The last thing I want is quantity over quality because that's what Jesus cares about. He cares about quality disciples who follow Him and follow the command in John 13:34-35 and 12-16. As we love others, we will desire to serve them as we serve our Lord. This is the primary reason I would rather discuss philosophy before Jesus, because if one does not agree with the Truth that is God's worldview, then they will not understand the purpose and nature of Himself.

I cannot stress how important it is to recognize this worldview and its prominence in millennial thinking. This is so crucial that one cannot function as a part of a local ministry without this understanding of Jesus being corrected. It is my desire that we, as followers of Jesus, take into consideration our current philosophies or world views so that we can match them up with God's definite reality of a factual creation in existence outside ourselves.

Please consider this prayerfully and focus on how Scripture talks about the world in which we live. Never once does

Scripture teach that what God has created can change based off our language use or perception.

It is my desire that we, as followers of Jesus, take into account our philosophies or world views so that they can match with the factual reality that God has created.

Please prayerfully consider not only my personal thoughts and view here but compare them with Scripture. Not once does Scripture talk about the single reality in which God has created as one that changes depending on the person's perception or word use about it. It is His desire that our philosophical views match His, don't fall into the traps of the world in which we live. What you hold may be valid, but not accurate.

CHAPTER 3

THE DESIGN

❖

"Church feels like a prison."

Picture a church with me. I imagine everyone will have their own base image of a building. Usually the building has open ceilings that point to the sky designed to make one think of heavenly things. Maybe it was a gothic cathedral with priceless stained-glass windows and multiple spires showing wealth and grandeur as a promise of what the Kingdom of God has in store for those who awe and desire to follow. Unfortunately, these are not church.

Church is wherever a group of people gather with the goal to know Jesus intimately by committing to serving and loving one another as He has first loved them. Simply put, this means Jesus followers that refuse to quit on one another (Acts 2:38-47, Matt 18:15-20). Now, I keep in tension this idea of refusing to quit with the idea that there will be those who claim to desire this but will only do so as long as it doesn't offend or inconvenience their lifestyle. When this happens, we must let them go for the good of the Church and welcome them as long as there is a repentant heart and the fruits of growth.

Does imagining that feel like a prison? A group of people designed to love each other and protect each other with such fierceness that others who look at them feel as if they're missing out in life. No, it doesn't feel like a prison. So why did I feel like this in local ministries my whole childhood?

To answer, let's consider chapter one and the problem that many millennials have faced, a lack of trust a disassociation with identity, and an unknown understanding of authority that is trustworthy. As information became more accessible, local ministries of Jesus followers have not done a fantastic job over the years of giving reasons as to why one ought to trust in the written Word and the Word Himself (John 1:1-18).

This issue lived out meant that "church" was inappropriate in learning how to communicate with me and love me as mindsets changed. It felt like prison to me because I did not know how to let the Holy Spirit affect my heart and actions as He designed. We are the only group able to love others that we would otherwise hate due to an external source that is beyond ourselves. This ability is a supernatural ability that only the Church can offer and Jesus followers can have (1 Cor. 13:4-8, 1 Jn. 4:7-15, Gal. 5:22-26).

❖

I would like to point out that my imagery and illustration here is one that equates the Church to a building set in the most amazing location imaginable, tight security on the doors, and windows that have impenetrable bars so that it's possible to see the beauty just beyond but never attain it fully. It is honest when we say the Church is set in the best location imaginable because where the church is, God is (Matt. 18:20). We are made the temple (Gal. 2:20 & Eph. 2:19-22). Often we in the States forget how sacred we are as Church and that we are literally designed to be His dwelling place, so much so that we are to live in a way that makes others want to be a part of it (Jn 13:35)!

Why have we made it feel as if there are high security locks on the doors of churches? Obviously, not all churches do this or feel like this when we become a part of them, but imagine an outsider with little sense of base identity and severe trust issues. Do you think they would walk in on a Sunday morning and feel like they're now part of a family in which they belong? I didn't. Sometimes I still don't and need to work at it to love them first so that the Holy Spirit can work in me and make me feel close to them as family through service. That happens sometimes, but what if it were a constant in any local body of Jesus followers? This is the standard Jesus calls us to and the Apostle Paul emphasizes in his letters (Eph. 4). The locks on the doors both keep people in and out of a prison. I have felt both in local bodies. Some are too easy to walk out of without being noticed, and some are too difficult to enter and be known. The locks on the doors only harm us.

On occasion, in scripture, we are warned that there will be "wolves in sheep's clothing," but when that happens we need to be aware and let them leave or tell them to for fear that may harm others (Matt. 7:15, Matt. 10:16). This is where leadership is called to be. In the middle of loving the group so much, they know and are able to discern who is not authentic. If ministries I had grown up in practiced this better, I would have seen groups of only honest, vulnerable Jesus followers who grew together as Jesus had designed. Are we doing this well in our ministries today, or are we too focused on retaining all those we can within the confines of our walls, our locks on our prisons?

In a cell I often picture a tiny window with firm bars. Unable to fit through the opening and unable to reach between them out to what is beyond, knowing I can never freely move. Are we doing this in our local bodies as leaders? In ministry, it is leadership's role to recognize, encourage, and empower others with their gifts. The window in this metaphor is being able to see the Kingdom of Heaven through the bars but not being able to engage in it fully, almost as a shadow of the desired product within itself. Simply a shadow of what it could be.

Where the Church is, there a footprint of the Kingdom is also. If we are truly the temple where Christ dwells and are able to maintain constant communication with Him, then others will be able to be a part of the Kingdom when they are with us in relationship whether they realize it or not. This in itself is a miracle. The last thing we should want is people to see us and engage with us and end up feeling as if the Kingdom we claim to be a part of is unattainable to the point our lives aren't changed as we claim. If that is the case, then we are not accurately reflecting the living Spirit within us, and this reflects poorly on the Kingdom.

In this window I also mentioned impenetrable bars. The bars here are symbolic of the people, especially leadership. Of course I am hesitant to be critical and accuse, but I often realize in the letters Paul wrote that he would even mention people and leaders by name! I do not claim to be Paul, nor will I mention people by name. However, as I stated in my preface, I desire for leadership to remain humble and willing to grow in reading this book. I also wrote that I desire for those under leadership reading this to not be divisive or create any issues for those in your body (including leadership). We are meant to be firm with one another but also never create an opening for the enemy, especially using criticism without being part of a solution. If you find yourself convicted here, pray about it, ask what God would have you do for your local ministry, and create ways to empower others in love so that they, and you, might grow.

In the metaphor, the bars on the window in the prison are when people show you glimpses of what the Kingdom on the other side is attached to but do not freely move or allow for movement within a meeting. This does not only take place on a Sunday morning but also in bible studies and other events/group gatherings throughout the week. I am not referring to the moments when people are helping each other in a time of need or where anointing happens spontaneously. Prayer for a person changes their life because they are allowing God to take control of an area. Those are the "good stuff moments" that show who and what we are. Consider a passage of scripture with me:

> *"And they devoted themselves to the apostles teaching and the fellowship, to the breaking of bread and the prayers. And awe came upon every soul, and many wonders and signs were being done through the apostles. And all who believed were together and had all things in common. And they were selling their possessions and belongings and distributing the proceeds to all, as any had need. And day by day, attending the temple together and breaking bread in their homes, they received their food with glad and generous hearts, praising God and having favor with all the people. And the Lord added to their number day by day those who were being saved." Acts 2:42-47 ESV*

Now read it one more time. If that does not astound you (it's reiterated in Acts 4 how they were like this as well), then I have no clue what will. In our harsh society, today, think back to the most socially alone mentioned in chapter one. There is no community that would not be appealing if they acted like this. There are select groups that do act this way to a large degree that attract millennials, and you won't like that the Church is not one that comes to mind. When I think about groups that love deeply, protect and care for one another, and spend days together because they desire to be with the people in them, cults, gangs, drug dens, sex clubs (or any community that misappropriates sexual appetites), and even bars come to mind. That is why people feel validated, drawn to, and accepted by them. All these have one thing in common, they center around a core idea, activity, or substance that brings them out of their current state of being.

Christ calls us to have Him as the center of our communities, and He creates with us and our community the Church, a state of being in the here and now that we are to love and be joyful in (Phil. 4:11-13). He brings us into community where we can become people who we want to be because we will be versions of ourselves that reflect only good traits. It is only our stubborn selfishness that gets in the way of this progressive work. If in the Church we become the bars through which one cannot fully experience all that the Kingdom of God has to offer, woe be to us, for we are doomed.

Let us not be like a prison putting locks on our doors and not letting those leave that need to and those seeking a righteous life because they see who we are as slaves of Christ enter. How dare we be as a prison, set in the best location on Earth (any realtor will tell you it is all about location, location, location) and not capitalize on the gifts God has given us through the grace of Christ and power of the Holy Spirit. Finally, let us be aware of the bars that can be the blocking force in being part of the Kingdom of Heaven so that we can make a gap big enough to be a part of the gateway rather than the window.

CHAPTER 4

ONE ANOTHER

❖

"Metaphors exist for a reason."

The family, body, bride.

There was a time when I was sitting in a coffee shop with a younger than I non-Christian to discuss why they had decided to become an atheist or agnostic after growing up in and around church. A question I was asked almost blew me away. We had gotten to the topic of scriptural inerrancy (in this person's mind there were many errors) when I was asked, "How does Jesus have a bride when He was never married?" Now, this was said with a tonality that was as if you had just checkmated someone's king in a game of chess. I, of course, remember thinking it was an absurd question but responded in kind with a certain phrase, "That is a metaphor." The Bible uses many of these.

The Bible is composed by many authors over a very long period of time. This means that as humans grow to understand the nature and character of God more, they use metaphors to help explain what they have learned and encountered. Metaphors create imagery to help describe something without being literal. The key word there is literal. Try reading Song of Solomon or Proverbs 31 sometime and picturing the description literally. Those become terrifying images instead of ones that are geared toward adoration. Almost every literary writing style is present in the single text that comprises the Bible.

Throughout the New Testament, as it was created by the Church for the Church (Paul wrote to specific local bodies and people but it still comes under the main definition from earlier in the book), we read about three main metaphors used to describe the Church. The first metaphor is as a family (Rom. 8:17, Eph. 1:4-5, & 1 Jn. 3:1-2, Col. 3:1). If then we are all made co-heirs with Christ, we ought to realize that to take part in the fruit, we must also bear fruit by taking part in the suffering. Christ calls us to suffer, though not of our own doing, but that the world will not accept us the more we seek after Him (Phil. 1:29, 3:8, Matt. 10:38, & 16:24, Rom 12:1-2). The metaphor of a family allows for us to understand how we are to treat one another as the blood of Christ is a thicker bond than the water of the womb.

The second metaphor we are given is as a body. Paul uses the metaphor of a body frequently to help the early Church realize how we are to be treated. Remember back to the fact that each individual is the temple. This means that you house the living God. You would not dare harm yourself when you hold this truth close. If you are all the temple, then you realize that you would not hurt others because you would treat others how you want to be treated (Luke 6:31, 1 Cor. 12:25-26). This is the metaphor that, right now, I am realizing we use most in the Church on average, but we are not living out.

The third metaphor is the one John the Baptist uses when he questioned a Jew who questioned him about the Messiah baptizing others in the Jordan. John had recently borne witness or declared that the Man in question was in fact the Messiah. The one they had been waiting for! He responds saying:

> "You yourselves bear me witness, that I said, I am not the Christ, but I have been sent before him.' The one who has the bride is the bridegroom. The friend of the bridegroom, who stands and hears him, rejoices greatly at the bridegroom's voice. Therefore this joy of mine is now complete. He must increase, but I must decrease.'" John 3:28-30 ESV

Notice the term John uses here, "bridegroom." If Christ is the bridegroom, we are the bride. We are to rejoice the same way John recognizes his need to. We also see this affirmed by the apostle John in the book of Revelation. He talks about the coming of the "lamb" (Jesus) and that His bride is to be ready (Rev. 19: 7). This is the metaphor I referenced at the beginning of this chapter. When we recognize how a husband is to love, cherish, and be the example to the wife, this metaphor takes on a deep meaning. Being the bride comes with the responsibility to care, guide, and show the love that is given to us to others. It's never meant to be kept selfishly, but in humility. How well are we at being the bride in waiting for a husband? Are we worthy enough of Him? I know I don't feel like we are at times.

❖

The body. As I stated previously, this is the metaphor that is hitting home for me. I find it absolutely crucial to understanding how we are to not make mistakes in the same way that the early Church did, hence the reason Paul had to write to them most of the time. He wrote letters of reproof (or correction) and encouragement, often times quite a mix of the two. In the single metaphor of the body we can realize how we are to treat one another, not treat one another, and how we are designed to function with one another. It is this functioning healthily idea that really gives me passion and is a driving force for this entire book. It is because I have become so in love with being a healthy body that I can no longer justify hurting one another the same way we hurt ourselves in sin.

We are to treat one another as we treat ourselves. Have you taken the time to look up all the new commands written in the New Testament for the Church that simply state "one another" or "each other" in them? If not, the list is extensive, and most condense it to around 65 verses total. I will reference a list at the end of the book that chooses 59 verses. This list mentions that "love one another" is repeated many times (and should scream how important that is)![2] I highly recommend you take a pause to go to the endnotes and prayerfully read through that list.

There are ones mentioned such as "do not grumble against" that I cannot help but read and think, "ouch." How often have I heard someone with their own agenda in a church gathering grumble against someone for getting in the way of their goal? This is unacceptable, and if we take the verse as a command like we ought to, then it's a sin! If this is going on, it needs to be noticed, corrected, and repented of.

To facilitate the behavioral process is the role of leadership. As a leader in a local body I find it difficult to do this in the moment it happens, especially in a group setting. It seems to come as a shock to those around that correction actually happens. If correction is needed it should not be left to leadership alone but accountability from the group itself.

With a body we are looking at treating one another as a single entity with Jesus as the head (Eph. 4:15-16). Paul writes about this in 1 Cor. 12, reminding us that we all have different gift and roles in a body. Still using the metaphor that each person is like a different part, a foot that helps us move, an ear that lets us hear, an eye that lets us see. Each one of the members are so crucial that if one cuts off the foot in a difference, disagreement or disappointment without reconciliation, then it is like cutting off one's own foot or gouging out an eye. It's gruesome but effective in helping us comprehend the importance of one another.

Imagine a group able to love one another as they love themselves so much so that in their desire of growth, they correct one another of wrong doings! If I claim to follow Jesus and know Him through a relationship, then I know He does not call us to stay as we are but to grow with Him and His body. In the human body there are white blood cells. They protect and activate when there are malicious attackers. If we at times recognize to be healthy (the only alternative is to die), then we need to be like the white cells that remove or correct those that do harm.

It is a tough reality to face that the Church is sacred. The word sacred is not one we use much anymore, even in evangelical Christianity. It's sad that the idea of something being sacred has lost meaning. Let's use a metaphor that I once heard: the presence of God being sacred is like the sun. The sun does good things as it provides life, feeds plants, gives light, and begins a new day. However, get too close, and like Icarus, you will feel its power. The sun, without protection, will burn if one spends too much time in its rays. This is the reason that the priests entering the holy of holies in the tabernacle or the temple had the chance of dying if they weren't ritually pure. Consider this passage:

> "And when they came to the threshing floor of Chidon, Uzzah put out his hand to take hold of the ark, for the oxen stumbled. And the anger of the Lord was kindled against Uzzah, and he struck him down because he put out his hand to the ark, and he died there before God. And David was angry because the Lord had broken out against Uzzah. And that place is called Perez-uzza to this day. And David was afraid of God that day, and he said, "How can I bring the ark of God home to me?" So

David did not take the ark home into the city of David, but took it aside to the house of Obed-edom the Gittite. And the ark of God remained with the household of Obed-edom in his house three months. And the Lord blessed the household of Obed-edom and all that he had." 1 Chronicles 13:9-14 ESV

Seems harsh at first. Without the proper understanding of what is sacred, the response to this passage is one that can make God seem harsh. But notice some key moments here. Uzzah did a seemingly good thing by stabilizing the ark to keep it from falling. However, he was not able to engage with the sacred in his current state. Although we do not necessarily know what his impure state was, we can look at David's reaction. First, we see anger, even to the point where the physical location was renamed to "breaking out against Uzzah."

Then it says David was afraid. Now, it is easy to think fear in the traditional sense as solely the emotion, but the word here is a deeper word in the Hebrew. This word is more akin to a healthy respect of or reverence. It is a concept that has been weeded out of vocabulary in a positive way. As a millennial, I remember a time when stranger danger was a common term, and fear was used to keep people safe (maybe too much so). Now, there is no positive sense in the word fear and any desire to teach respect or reverence comes with an inherent lack of trust towards the idea and the person sharing it when there ought to be fear or reverence only because you understand you are loved. Think about 1 John 4:18. We can understand that David knew what this meant truly when we see his response to not take the ark into his own city. Obed-edom is mentioned later as a place that stored treasures of the king (2 Ch. 25:24).

When the Bible talks about the body of Christ being a new temple, it should bring to mind a sense of reverence and deep respect for those who carry the living God in them, including yourself. The weight of the Church and how sacred it is treated is on the believer individually. It needs to be treated as sacred as the ark. Recall a moment in Acts 5 with Ananias and Sapphira who lie to their local body about how much money they will give after selling a property they own. Individually, each one lies, and both, one after the other, are killed on the spot for it by the Spirit. This is meant to show us that there are consequences for profaning the sacred.

How are we doing at treating each other and breeding ways for deep connection to happen so that we can love and respect each other as deeply as Christ did with the first twelve disciples? I can only assess myself and my heart with my local body. It is entirely up to you as the reader to be honest in prayer about this yourself. If this leads to conviction, ask where and how you can be part of the solution. May we as sacred temples grow and treat others as if we care about our own bodies.

CHAPTER 5

A CALL TO TRANSPARENCY

❖

"We need to remove things that communicate distrust."

I remember when I was in a rural community southern Baptist Church growing up. Tight knit family, great food after service, and fun programs for kids. It was in that ministry that I recall my brother, late at night, asking questions full of doubt and misconceptions about scriptural truth. Those sessions with the pastor at the time were ones that would leave him with a lack of proper theological understanding and constant frustration. There was a specific moment in his questioning process and understanding that he told me heaven was a bunch of people singing praises to God for all eternity and then said, "Does that sound fun to you?"

My young Jesus loving brain saw no problems with that image. However, now that I am older, I realize the problem here: He was reading scripture or going off what others had told him without understanding the richness behind it. This only means one thing; it was not being taught in a way that was accurate and biblical.

I tell this story to help us realize that there are many people like this who hold random biblical half-truths that allow them to have reasoning as to why the Christian faith is incompatible with logic. Communication is everything. In this chapter we will discuss what we do as the Church currently that communicates trust, distrust, and how we might be able to remedy this for the millennial and later generations. Let us not be ones who share half-truths with others, especially about the Bible and our own lives.

"Folk theology" is a term that I first heard in college. Simply defined it means biblical teachings that are not accurate to scripture. For example, the teaching that one must turn the other cheek and not stand up for one's self is accurate to scripture. This is false. When Jesus is saying this, He lists it in other moments that say how to show someone else that they are making wrong choice and abusing others. After this verse there is one that says if asked to give your coat, give not only your coat but all other clothes as well. Essentially, strip yourself naked and bring them shame (Matt. 5:38-48). It is so dangerous to take verses and phrases out of context for this exact reason. This can hurt the body immensely to not understand the heart and character of God when teaching the Bible to others.

How often would you imagine you hear about "folk theology" on a Sunday morning service? I recon not very often. It is this lack of transparency in saying we may be wrong about certain things the church has upheld as truth for years that creates an outside perspective of distrust and Christian bigotry. We need to remain humble and teachable. Especially leadership in local bodies. It is my desire that we recognize our short comings as Jesus followers and apologize for the perception that we are always right. The Church first must be followers of Jesus living as told in obedience before telling others what we might think we know as fact before we discern for ourselves.

The millennial generation has an inherent lack of trust and an infinite wealth of knowledge at their fingertips. This idea alone should scare the Church into desiring discipleship maturity and wanting to know the Living God they serve through His written word. It was recommended at first to counter this with pure reliance on personal testimony and experience saying, "It was real to me." This has sense stopped working due to what I mentioned previously in chapter two about philosophy. It is no longer sufficient for us to go off of personal experience alone but to explain biblical truths with a matter of confidence and willingness to share that your current understanding may be inaccurate. Share your vulnerabilities in confidence.

It is basic level human instinct to respond to how vulnerable someone is with you in mind. If someone communicates a vulnerability and becomes transparent with you, you are left with two options. The first option is to be uncaring (usually disguised as sympathy). The second is to empathize by putting yourself in their place and wanting to show them that they are loved (usually by responding with a vulnerability of your own to let them know they are not alone). It is in these moments that you have the chance to show who you really are.

There are severe consequences if we do not practice this in the Church. Imagine if people claiming to love one another did not share faults openly so that they could grow and change to be healthier people. To an outsider that would look pretty hypocritical, right? Thank goodness we don't do that behavior today!

I find it no accident that James 5:13-20 says that healings will happen when the soul confesses and repents, but even more so that in the soul healing process we need to confess our faults or sins to one another as a practice. The good news is, even though it may be uncomfortable and difficult for both parties, it gives a sense of relief and way to love more deeply. When we surrender our wants, desires, and unhealthy practices there is freedom that follows. The freedom is under a master that teaches you how to be the best version of yourself, not a slave to sin which leads to death (John 8:31-38). It is in community that builds trust and openness for which people hunger.

❖

At this point the question that needs to be answered is, "What are we doing that communicates distrust?" Aside from the biblical literacy that is commonplace in Church today and the lack of vulnerability, there are actions that many local bodies hold that communicate distrust. The primary actions that have kept others with a perception of distrust have to deal with three things: finances, poor leadership, and slow willingness to adaptation of change.

$Money$

In the ministries that treat the Church like a business there are always concerns of finances being abused. I think of the largest ministries with Jesus Jets and campuses with facilities in different cities. One could argue that these means provided justify the end goal. I am only an outsider of analyzing mega churches (though I've visited I've never been in the leadership of one). I have a difficult time understanding the fact that mega ministries thrive in the first place.

Recall what we have discussed so far as the role of the Church and the need for trust. There are many large ministries that become safe havens for those who come wanting to be fed but not be known. This is a mentality that is antithetical to the nature of being a loving body of Christ. Mega churches are often fortresses of refuge for those who don't want to be found.

Misuse of financial gains are not from mega churches alone (of course not every one of them either) but also from small ministries. I was once a part of a small ministry in a vacation town that only had a core of about 15-20 people. On a Sunday service there were about 60 plus. I won't say much more other than what I know was an unfortunate mistreatment of finances from people that were unable to keep the body accountable. It is ministries such as these that create a perception that is negative toward the image of Church as a whole.

I propose as a way to eliminate a chance of mistrust and the perception (leave no room for the appearance of evil), that we remove all things money is spent on that is superfluous. For each local ministry this may look different. For some it may be removing a building, for others it may be keeping the building and removing any paid leadership. I cannot say. I can, however, say that we need to take this into serious prayer and consideration with our elder boards and ask God, "If we remove [x], are we still willing to serve you?" What are you least willing to get rid of and stop paying for? Will that define the Church or is it the people that comprise it? I think you can see where this is leading. Christ often asks us to exit our comfort zones, finances are simply one more way to stay comfortable. May we be able to analyze our hearts and local ministries honestly taking outside perceptions into account.

Poor Leadership, is it I?

As a leader in a local body, this section will contain thoughts that wake me up at night. Whenever I consider that what leadership does reflects on a local ministry, I become immediately concerned. In our current culture negative news is what spreads like wildfire. It is not often that I hear people or news stations discuss positive topics. Have you thought about why this is? It's because we gravitate toward things that shock us and are unexpected. We gravitate towards evil. Evil and hearing about it has become the new normal that we are now increasingly desensitized by. If good is expected and commonplace, then unfortunately, we consider it as normal. Good should be something noticed and celebrated instead of taken for granted. The fact that we give evil attention ought to scare us.

I bring this to attention under the leadership section because if we in leadership act as if our sins and wrongdoings will go unnoticed, we are sorely mistaken. I think back to the 1980's and the boom of televangelist preachers that would misuse their roles and stage acts of God for show. In this time period a lot of credibly was lost because of a few. That is the impact leadership has as the "face" of the Church. At that point, the outside perspective is only a minor concern to how many relationships a leader has the potential to destroy with others and with Jesus from within.

I grieve for those hundreds of thousands and more whose relations with Jesus and others have been wrecked due to a leader not yielding to the heart of God in the moment. Around the local body I serve, we use what is called the two-sentence prayer. Try it as you read it. Take it slow. Repeat each sentence three times and choose a noun to focus on.

> "Lord, let me see [my local ministry] as you see them. Lord, let me feel for [my local ministry] as you feel for them."

Now try the prayer with your name as the focus. Say this prayer with an open heart and open mind. What did God show you? Was it perhaps that you are His child and that He has nothing but love for you? Maybe some love mixed with a sense of conviction over heart conditions not repented for? Those are usually a mix of all of them for me when I pray this in my own life. I have Pastor V. Lee Gregory to thank for making this prayer more simple and concise than anywhere I've heard it before. He gives permission for this to be shared and utilized as much as possible.

This prayer is one of the best tools in a leader's tool belt to best serve the Kingdom of God. His body, bride, and family need leaders who will first be confident in knowing that there are infinite reasons to serve from humility. We must remain humble. Paul writes:

> "But though we had already suffered and been shamefully treated at Philippi, as you know, we had boldness in our God to declare to you the gospel of God in the midst of much conflict. For our appeal does not spring from error or impurity or any attempt to deceive, but just as we have been approved by God to be entrusted with the gospel, so we speak, not to please man, but to

please God who tests our hearts. For we never came with words of flattery, as you know, nor with a pretext for greed—God is witness. Nor did we seek glory from people, whether from you or from others, though we could have made demands as apostles of Christ. But we were gentle among you, like a nursing mother taking care of her own children. So, being affectionately desirous of you, we were ready to share with you not only the gospel of God but also our own selves, because you had become very dear to us. For you remember, brothers, our labor and toil: we worked night and day, that we might not be a burden to any of you, while we proclaimed to you the gospel of God. You are witnesses, and God also, how holy and righteous and blameless was our conduct toward you believers. For you know how, like a father with his children, we exhorted each one of you and encouraged you and charged you to walk in a manner worthy of God, who calls you into his own kingdom and glory. And we also thank God constantly for this, that when you received the word of God, which you heard from us, you accepted it not as the word of men but as what it really is, the word of God, which is at work in you believers."
1 Thessalonians 2:2-13 ESV

I know it's a long section, but it's worth the read. Realize in this passage Paul lays out that they were bold with the Gospel, thankful that it was received, and worked in their community to provide for themselves as servants that they might not be a burden. This single passage in combination with Titus 1 and 1 Tim. 3 are the prime examples of what leadership qualities need to be and how that can be lived out. Take this passage and look at what needs to be exemplified in leadership. It is by God's grace alone that we are given the ability to serve and it is a privilege to share the Gospel message. Do not forget the reason why we are called and to the whom we are called. They never came to Thessalonike (now modern-day Thessaloniki) to live there and make money out of greed or seek glory from others, but so that they might help raise the community to spiritual maturity. If this is not our goal as leaders today, then may we be corrected and convicted enough to abandon our positions and become right with God or repent and change our hearts and ways. Our ways of communicating our repentance or stepping down to not be lukewarm will display that we can be trusted in ways that we once might have been too proud to admit.

Slow willingness to change

In relation to recognition of leadership being held accountable, we as the Church are also to be held accountable. We as a body, bride, and family need to display that we are trustworthy also. Abandon the pride, destroy the ego, and let Jesus take over as the head. After this, we might discover that what remains will be those that desire to seek after Him with all they have to offer.

Jesus gave us the command to love one another as fiercely as He has loved us without quitting. We cannot first do that without emptying ourselves individually and giving over to Him. Where we once thought we were important in our own right, we must diminish. Where we once were given status by others, we must let our status only come from Him. Our pride and our individual egos keep us from fulfilling this commandment. How selfish can we get?! Are you kidding me?! No wonder people look at the Church designed to love each other and think hypocrite. Jesus says, "He'd rather us be hot or cold to Him but not lukewarm or He'd rather spit us out of His mouth" (Rev. 3:16 & Matt. 12:30). This is another one of those thoughts designed to wake us up at night and keep us motivated to fulfill that command.

If this is us individually and collectively, we must ask for forgiveness! However, Christ never simply allows us to repent and forget, but we retain memories in hopes that we might change as led by His Spirit. Every moment that we repent and do not change our ways is another way for us to fall back into old habits and need to repent again out of pain and disappointment. We are called to change and progress in our sanctification, even as a Church. Often this is discussed individually, but if we are a single body. Should it not be the same?

As local structures, we often get into habits and structures entrenched into thought patterns. Concerns that change might mean people leave or needing to consult every single person on the membership roster. I am not saying these are bad things to consider, but I am saying they impede the process. How dare we slow down what God is telling us to do as local bodies or individuals? Having an elder board that is the spiritual overseeing group is essential to the local ministry. In reference to leadership they must be willing to first serve the will of God and what is best for others even if we do not like the change.

God often tells us to grow and change outside of our comfort zones. If we do not like the change put into effect, we must learn to grow with it and love through it. There will always be those who consider that the "last straw" and leave. Either let them or confront them as to why, and challenge them to stay spiritually (do not let this role fall on leadership alone). If you care about those with this heart condition, challenge them to stay because you love them and the body needs their uniqueness. Otherwise let them go until they are repentant for divorcing the body. A person is either leaving a local body because they are selfish and judgmental, or they think leadership does not care about them.

Let us not be slow to change. Let our elders be open, honest, and vulnerable with each other as leadership. Let us listen, repent, and enact the will of God in our local ministries. Let us not impede the work of Holy Spirit in our ministries and personal lives. In our virtue degrading culture, we must show what the correct definition of love is through being the body, bride, and family we are designed to be. Give us a reason to trust ourselves in our obedience to Jesus and others will begin to trust who we are without us having to seem convincing.

CHAPTER 6

REPENTANCE

❖

"A repentant heart leads to change."

To have guilt and understand grace is a blessing that we as members of the Jesus following community get the privilege of having in abundance. The living Holy Spirit within us gives us the ability to know what is right and know what is wrong (Jn 16:8). Feeling guilt is often a fact that He is still working in one's life. It is necessary to know that this can be one of our biggest strengths in relationships with one another and with those who are not part of the Church. As Jesus followers we are left the charge of living in agreed upon subjection to serving God. The rest of the world is not so fortunate.

One thing we were reminded of in the previous section is the fact that forgiveness is required to restore broken relationships. This also means that repentance must happen to complete true mending on both sides. Jesus warned His followers about what would happen if they did not initiate the forgiveness process (Matt 6:14-15).

Many books have been written on repentance and forgiveness alone because of how saturated with Scripture the theme is. In all of Jesus's discussions about repentance, one story stands out the most. Let us recall the story of the prodigal son (Luke 15:11:32). In this famous parable Jesus refers to a son who takes his early inheritance before his father's time and abuses the gift by living a life of debauchery until he is left with nothing. This is the moment we will focus on. Having nothing, this young man decides to at least work as a free hand on a pig farm eating what little slop food the pigs don't. He hit an all-time low in his life. Recognizing this, he thinks, "Let me go and see if I can be a servant for my dad because their lives are much better than mine." Here is our key moment in the story. His life had to land flat on its back, broken and shattered before he was willing to ask for repentance.

I mentioned previously that we are not willing to let people go and their lives to be broken before they reach the point of repentance often enough in local ministries and the Church. This is a big problem. The next point that comes from this is that we as the Church are not very apologetic to the people we hurt in every level of the body, not only the leadership. I implore you, if you are a Jesus follower, to ask and consider those that the Church has hurt and apologize for the pain that we have caused as a representative to the culture at large. You are an ambassador for Christ and the Church, if you are in discussions with others and they disclose that they no longer believe because of harm in a Church, you are allowed to apologize.

We ought not apologize for the fact that we have a personal relationship with Jesus. If someone has been hurt by the Church or because of a specific local body and you find all the details may be accurate, there are grounds for us to repent. We will not repent for our beliefs but only acts that harm others. My greatest concern in writing this is that it will give others an excuse to apologize for people's inaccurate perceptions of how they were hurt by a local body and say that their local body is better than the one they came from. The mentality of "church hopping" should be widely discouraged. If a local congregation doesn't have the style of music or the amenities you prefer, discuss with leadership why not and see if you can be part of making that change happen. Depending on the reason, it may not be grounds enough to leave the local body that you partnered with.

Disagreement is not grounds for divorce. There is a sincere difference between repenting on legitimate grounds and repenting because their perception of how they were hurt is inaccurate to what actually happened. I desire for the Church to be able to say we are sorry for truly hurting others, but if they leave of their own accord and restoration cannot be made, we have a word for that. Abandonment. It is one of the few reasons that divorce may happen on biblical grounds, but that does not make it an acceptable response. I bring this up because in our process in letting people that hurt the body go, we need to hold in tension that true Jesus followers need to be willing to sacrifice their wants and desires for the good of a local body. Remember back to Acts that gratitude should come from a place of love in the body of Christ, so we should be serving from a place of love. That is what makes the community God designed tick and become attractive to those who do not know Him.

Some things we as the Church are allowed to repent to the culture for are: the example for Jesus followers that we have set, the allowance of hypocrisy to stay within local bodies for whatever reason, and that Christians have committed atrocities in the name of Jesus calling themselves righteous in the process. Biblical text has been abused and manipulated for centuries to say what the reader desires it to say as opposed to what it says in its original intended meaning. Reading Scripture in context is crucial to understanding who the person of God is in Father, Son, and Holy Spirit. That is why when it was translated from Latin into the people's language, it was enough to incite a revolution. People had finally understood what was being misused in the text to hurt them instead of helping them. Every Christian hates to bring up the crusades in history, but shouldn't we be the first to apologize to those in other faiths? For those cultures, Christ is still a bad name that brings up horrific murder scenes.

❖

Imagine having a church culture where we are willing to repent to those whom we have wronged immediately when we find out about it. This is the standard we are called to. It would immediately change the perception of those within our local bodies. Those people would then affect all the other's in their lives. We as Jesus followers not only need to forgive but to repent faster than any other people group. This mentality, if adopted well, would lead to the biggest change in Church culture. Once we can repent, others have the newfound opportunity to forgive.

I will never forget the first time I asked a family member who was not a Jesus follower why they didn't believe. It was a short but seemingly well thought out answer that stated with a couple of other beliefs about theories that disprove the Bible. Those theories at the beginning were not the real reason why they chose not to believe in Christ (I've found it usually takes some digging to get the real heart of the reason). In questioning their story, I learned one crucial thing. A leader had said something not necessarily needed for salvation that they disagreed with, which in turn harmed the family and that leader never sought to seek why or ask for forgiveness. Granted my family member never asked clarifying questions (that I know of). However, Church culture never created a comfortable space where they felt safe asking questions.

We have removed choice of belief from Church culture. It is completely acceptable to be ready to ask questions so that one might know the answer (1 Peter 3:15). As humans we are given the ability to believe in Jesus. The apostles are asked in Matthew 16:13-20 after a crowd walks away, "Who do you say that I am?" This is the single most important question that a human will ask about Jesus in their life. Allowing the freedom of choice as part of our Church curriculum, especially for teens, is exponentially important. It garners respect when we can say, "You don't have to believe what we teach you, but we can tell you why we believe Jesus is the Son of God, cleansed us of our sins by death, and rose again as the eternal king." When we remove choice of belief, we drive people away as the Church.

Consider the last two to three major generations of Church going folk. They have dwindled to single digit percentiles because they were not provided a safe space for questioning and belief. There are plenty verses to teach us that faith is not going to be proven until given to subjection under God's authority (Hebrews 11:1). Faith is something that needs room for growth into trust and cannot grow when told that one cannot question its origin. It may start as small as a mustard seed but still ought to be cultivated. Removal of choice and told lines such as, "because I said so" no longer work with people in an information laden world.

As we aim to create a repentant Church culture, change will follow. Repentance starts with us and asking how we can not only ask for forgiveness, but how we can live rightly in obedience to Christ. Let us not forget the Holy Spirit's role in our personal lives as well as our collective local bodies.

I know this is not an easy task. To change the culture within a local body seems impossible at times. It is up to leadership to begin living it out and sharing their actions and how it has affected them verbally. Let us be honest in asking if others feel safe to question and how we can facilitate the growth process so as not to drive people away by being closed about why we believe what we believe.

CHAPTER 7

CHURCH, AGAIN

❖

"It is my desire to be Church, again."

"I don't want to go to church again." I remember a time in my younger life when I said that sentence to my dad. I meant it. Remember the prison metaphor? No kid would want that. As a millennial, I know we can become Church, again. As we have defined prior, being Church means that we are able to live out God's design in loving one another as He has loved us, and are able to be transparent about not only who we are, but why we believe what we believe in humility with clear communication. There is richness in this world that only the Church has access to through the Holy Spirit dwelling in us. God gave us one reality in which we get one chance to be the best human we can be. Don't let it go to waste.

In this book I have mentioned some topics that are not new. In fact, I would like to attribute a lot of this to what I have learned and gleaned from others as well as the Bible. I bring the millennial conversation to the table because the future people that are going to be attracted to Church are the millennials, if we live it right. In our online community building culture, we are missing communities that stay together because they are committed to love each other and not break off and divorce to start new ones because of disagreement.

If time is the essence of life. We cannot afford to be slow to change any longer, because as we waste time, others are killing their time in ways that are suicidal. I will not claim to know what is best for your local body in ways to help change the culture, but I can say what I am doing to help. I have begun a four-part class that requires us to discuss topics we disagree on. As people enter or join the group, others leave because they find it too difficult. We have agreed to the syllabus which requires us to be transparent as we go through the Bible, doctrines, spiritual practices, and practical ways of living out what is being taught. In this class people have had to wrestle together, and in doing so, have grown closer together. This has been fairly close to a group of believers as described when we discuss the makeup of Church. In this group I am even able to assess an individual's gifting and potential leadership qualities. If you are curious about this long-term class, contact me via email address listed at the end of the book.

Ever since I began ministry, I have asked the question to Jesus, "How do I church plant a church within a church?" I now realize that this is a misguided question. Instead I am needing to give a local body a reason to become Church, again. A group of people such as the class becomes an example to the rest of the local body when they start showing growth and change. They will then teach and share with others the growth that they've been experiencing.

I was inspired by reading *Letters to the Church* by Francis Chan to write about this topic from a millennial in ministry's perspective.[3] After reading that book, which pairs well with a deeper insight into the desires I mention here, I remember him saying that he was able to start *We Are Church* as a new model, but changing an already existing local body's culture is going to be a lot more difficult. I think that, we as the Church in the United States and other western society, can change and grow. Don't let this design for Church only exist in new "church plants," but let it start with you as a member or a leader. In the wrong hands this can be used for divisiveness, I will never condone that and neither does God. Be cautious when caring deeply. Let it not be my words or Francis Chan's words or anyone else's that you weigh heavy on but on the Scriptures. Double check facts, seek wisdom, and stay humble in constant prayer.

As I write this, I can honestly say, I want to be Church and that means I have to go where others who are Church are as well. The word "church" has been so abused and misused as it was never intended. Leadership has allowed this to happen by calling a local body and a place to go, "church." Like a restaurant, you go because you're hungry, but you might not find one that's "good" and may even give you food poisoning. Now that we have redefined Church appropriately it is time for us to be Church, again, I desire to be Church, again.

PHILOSOPHICAL VIEW:

A Dive into a Synoptic Vision

To understand the beginning of my journey of a synoptic vision, one should understand what a synoptic vision is and wonder about the environment around them and how it affects who they are as a being. [4] Honestly, it was a difficult task coming up with a definition, and that is not to say that it could not have been achieved, but my peer, Shawn Colacchia's, [5] was phenomenal and much more effective at portraying the heart of a synoptic vision. In this reading, I will attempt to provide a view that has begun with wonder and its exploration.

So thusly we shall begin this journey using the imagination. Picture, for a moment, that one is under the sea, waves reflecting the sun downwards as beams of light. It is calming. There is no need for air, no need to breathe, everything is quiet, and one feels at peace. There is only a need to explore and explore one shall.

Now, because we have an active imagination, we can still get a grasp of what this reality will be. Looking down below, there is a wrecked vessel half embedded in the sand, showing corrosion and growth of new life as the ages have passed along. It looks to be teeming with an abundance of various forms of sea life; there are small schools of fish, the occasional hunting shark, plenty of coral and kelp surrounding the vessel, the opportune spot to dive deeper into what one knows and what one wants to know. Being wary and curious, one approaches with caution. Towards the bow of the former ship, the wood has been splintered. Long ago it cracked into a hole which, due to decay, is now large enough to swim through. Inside the hole one finds that the ship is much deeper than one had originally thought. A second deck is below, unnoticed, from outside. Once, a resplendent trade ship, the markings of corrosion and decay has settled on the barrels of alcohol, which have remained trapped in their watery tombs. Human curiosity kicks in as a spooked octopus squirts out ink, quickly jetting away. There is one barrel still tightly sealed that draws attention and beckons one closer. Worried to touch it in fear it might crumble, but still exceptionally curious, one reaches out their hand to investigate the barrel further. Observing that although time has passed, it remains sturdy, resilient to the unending pressure of the water; it is surprising that perceptions can be wrong. One thinks to one's self that this barrel is real, as the barrel did not change no matter the perception (the way one chooses to view the world).[6] This is how one perceives the world when they focus on the understanding of the objects around them, being tangible regardless of how language is used. Worldview is a construct of perception to create a synoptic view of analyzing and looking at the world. This can be understood through the means of science, thought, and observation. [7] Moving away, allowing the barrel to remain undisturbed, one decides to move on to the next room. During the transition, a buzzing noise occurs as a fuzzy voice trickles down into the communication device on one's head.

A marine research biologist speaks into the ear bud and asks what one has discovered on the underwater adventure thus far. The appropriate response is sent up to the receiver above from the diver. "To see reality as anything but the world around us is, in my opinion, foolish. There are blatant signs around us that this is a designed world to show us what is beyond ourselves so that we may take notice of our perception of others." Moments later, the somewhat metallic sound continued. "It is differentiating between the terms that is going to explain why I believe in an objective reality. To establish what a realist believes before continuing: "Realists believe that no entity has its primary features, even in part, dependent on the human perception of them, even though humans may be related to them." [8] This perception can be upheld about anything physical such as a leaf or grain of sand to an idea such as liberty. Perception meaning the way one chooses to view the world. One may perceive the world whichever way they like, but that will not change the world, or reality itself. Paul says in his letter to the Romans, "For his invisible attributes, namely, his eternal power and divine nature, have been clearly perceived, ever since the creation of the world, in the things that have been made. So they are without excuse."[9] This is a spiritual approach to how concrete this world is, because it is all to show us the glory of one bigger, and our perception will not change the perception that it was made with. This idea, when compared with one such as sense experience, makes little to no reason, simply because when one believes that they can only use their physical senses to come to an understanding of it, one may begin to believe that they may feel the need to scale a mountain to know that its peak is in existence. Whether or not one has an informed opinion (a view, judgment, or appraisal formed in the mind about a particular matter)[10] is not to be determined by one's self, but to be left up to another determiner, for one can think they have done well but in fact, less than succeeded in their task." I have my opinion based upon foundations from, many with reasoning."

The crackling voice from above comes back to life, saying, "I'm glad you do not agree with Jacques Derrida. As the father of postmodernist thinking, Derrida was a relativist[11] in his philosophy, making argumentation difficult to agree on the same beliefs. Please continue feeding back information about what you have learned, as it helps form an understanding of the world around us."

"Aye, sir."

Moving on upstairs into the crew quarters, the desolate hammocks look lonely fixed upon the walls. A place once full of life is now empty and awash with loneliness. It makes one wonder what had happened. Feeling a warm current flow through the quarters, it wraps around one's body in a gentle embrace, killing the feelings of loneliness and the emptiness one feels within this room. A reminder of loved ones, both present and past as the gentle sway of the water rocks one's body in a motion of tender care. A soft whisper of the gentle love like that of a mother rocking their child to sleep.

On the portside wall is an etched symbol of the cross. A bible lesson about ethics, virtue, and the fruits of the spirit comes to mind. The understanding of virtue in relation to the world, meaning that when looking at societal issues it is how one understands what is right and wrong or virtuous and evil. For further human flourishing, the best of humanity is created out of virtue within ethics.

A soft, quiet crackle comes over the speakers down below, "what an interesting concept. Where does the idea of asking a question lead to the manifestation of it?"

"Evil exists through a lack of virtue, thus virtue and evil are in a reciprocated relationship so that if one exists, so does its counterpart. When someone asks if evil exists, it is there because humans are not choosing to follow the best possible way of life. Failing to reach or attempting to reach the greatest of opportunities presented either through lack of wisdom, personal will, or any other reason is what leads to the creation of evil."

"Oh, so you are saying that not only not reaching the best opportunities and paths are evil, but also not striving for that place in the world is evil too?"

"Yes."

"Good work, continue radioing back when you have more to discuss."

"Will do."

Continuing to swim along, one finds the galley just up ahead and notices a bottle hanging from the ceiling. It has been crusted over and the liquid inside distorts the rest of the room behind it. Taking a minute to ponder and examine this change and what the room actually looks like behind the bottle one wonders the reality of truth. Still not actually realizing the thoughts are being vocalized and heard over the scratchy intercom system one continues to think out loud saying, "Truth, it is certainly a bigger concept than one might assume. One without distortion such as this bottle in front of me seems to do. Something that is unable to be incorrect (or false). The realist view of truth is that which is objectively independent of how we perceive the object as well as independent from our thoughts or claims about the world. [12] There are multiple theories of truth, however; such as the pragmatic and postmodern theories of truth.[13] These are certainly intriguing, but do not seem to hold the weight that lets all know what really is beyond belief. This definition, with Jesus' philosophy of truth, according to John, "Then you will know the truth, and the truth will set you free."[14] I believe is powerful. Due to the nature of truth being able to set one's mind free from anything holding the person back is well worth the pain of discovering. In objective reality, as stated previously, it states simply at one point; the object does not change no matter the perception.[15] There is a point where one ought to take notice of the two in correlation. What is true for me is also true for everyone else when it comes to the way the world works. One should know a number "5" in the business world as the number "5" any other number such as a "6" regardless of whoever is taking inventory still would need that number to be a "5" regardless of belief. Otherwise the company will have stock-inventory will be wrong and as a repercussion, one might get fired or the company will go out of business provided this mode of thinking continues. To know how to be a good person, one ought to know what that looks like in the world, not what that is according to their own belief system. As opposed to the postmodernist anti-realist philosophy where one decides all their own beliefs as according to them and how they interpret the world.[16] One of the more worrisome modes of this line of thinking to me is that where is the boundary? One that says murder and rape are wrong (for me), but maybe not wrong at all for my neighbor and if she/he wanted to do them, they may be permissible. These are the things one cannot be certain about if they do not know the truth. To keep from chaos in society, I hereby conclude truth is objective and absolute."

Crackling back through the earpiece once again is a single word, "wow."

"Oh! You heard all that?"

"Very much so." The reply came. The voice continued to say, "I very much am curious what someone would say about how one may know this for certain."

"Well, knowledge is that which someone discerns and understands, true or not[17]; they have learned through either logical argumentation (i.e. Syllogisms)[18] or experience. There are multiple types of knowledge, however, they all lead to some form of comprehension. Therefore, if one is able to test something against reality and allow objectivity to be engrained in their understanding they may be able to find the truth about the concept or object much more easily than if it were to be open to interpretation, making more sense in interpersonal relationships to discuss a topic in common understandings and seeking of the truth about what it is. Like this bottle before me. It can be discussed because our understanding of it is not subjective and we can further analyze and seek the truth about it."

"Ah, that makes a lot of sense, just by discussing under the same understanding we are able to know the object and our views about it as well as each other's beliefs and understanding of the world much better"

"Correct."

After some time passes there is another crackle and the voice begins to speak further. "What about us? How are we supposed to know who we are?"

"Well, that is the question of a lifetime, is it not? I guarantee that answer will continue to change with you and will always need to be addressed; however, it does not mean that it is impossible to do so."

"So, I feel the question is begged, will you try?"

One takes a deep breath and replies with a single word, "Yes." Floating around in thought and in the water a moment while a small fish enters the room, then just as abruptly leaves again, the long-awaited reply begins. "To feel, and more importantly to love, over all else. In psychology it is proven that emotion has a necessary place in the human psyche. What happens when we take the knowledge gained here and use it to help us understand ethics in philosophy? The topic of ethics is quite an important one. It attempts to answer questions such as, 'am I a good person?' 'How can I be a good person?' and most importantly, 'What is a good person?' I have been able to make several well put together arguments that to begin asking what "good" is and how we can adapt these qualities into our lives is through the beauty of virtue which I have come to understand as:

Virtue ethics (as opposed to virtue epistemology) is the focus of how virtue is used interpersonally and since we have an interpersonal world, this is the one I will focus on. Ethically, virtue is, morally valuable in a character trait or much more deeply engrained into one's being than that. It deals "with emotions and emotional reactions, choices, values, desires, perceptions, attitudes, interests, expectations and sensibilities. To possess a virtue is to be a certain sort of person with a certain complex mindset."[19] Most people derive their ideas from Aristotle's claim that a virtuous person is in who has ideal character traits.[20]

Marrying this idea of virtue to emotions: First, we should notice within ourselves why we want to be virtuous people. I claim that the highest overall virtue in existence is love and that no one in existence, except for a pure, virtuous being could be the source of that love for our universe and humanity is flawed. Second, after establishing the previous couple of sentences above, one should see how their emotions play in their decision making and daily life choices. Do they add to your virtue? Probably not always, though to be like God, that is what we strive to do, make actions based upon virtuous qualities within ourselves out of a loving heart.

Regardless, the point here is that we, as humans, are hopefully trying. Next, we ought to establish that emotions are not inherently evil, like power or money, for example, evil may be drawn to these things more often than not, but it is not evil to have money or power, it is how you use it. Emotions are the same as this, anger is not a bad thing it can simply be used for evil or misused entirely and directed at the wrong thing (or worse, person). C.S. Lewis discusses in *The Abolition of Man* that to cut ourselves off from our emotions, in fact, makes us less human and more like your average Vulcan (Spock type figure from *Star Trek*). To combine all these concepts allows for the foundation of a person to take a healthy step in the direction of helping one's self and spreading truth and love to others and future generations. No matter where your emotions come from or how they occur, let us start to understand ourselves better from them and in doing so, understand the world around us."

"You're saying all that makes me wonder why I live. Why I try to be and care about being a healthy person. Why is it worth the effort?" The now familiar crackle sends these questions in a tone that makes it sound as though the voice the words are coming from is looking for assurance and some what aloft.

Understanding well what asking those questions is like and coming to realizations being an important part of the growth process is a large part of why one has decided to live the way they do. Contemplating the response, one answers assuredly, "These answers to your questions can be made from what we have discussed but one cannot answer them for you. It should be done only by you and your thoughts."

Hearing this the only thing one receives back is a loving, "thank you."

That "thank you" is what one lives for. Helping others come to terms with their wondering and embracing it so that they may have the grounds to now form thoughts for one's self out of love and wanting to love. Minus the captain's cabin and what treasures it may hold, this sunken vessel has been thoroughly explored and one cares not for the possible riches of this world, that conversation was all one needed. It was spoken from the heart out of truth, love, and virtue. One could not have asked for a better dive into the soul. Into a connection that may have been a once in a lifetime event, an event of pure beauty. Just as beautiful as the teaming life around in this seemingly perfect environment. Exiting the ship and looking up from where one started a sudden realization occurs. One is not alone and has thousands more experiences and explorations to make. All for the purpose of growth, love, and purpose in this peaceful yet hectic world. This wonder that begins in us all.

One takes a last look around and sees the filtered light through the water illuminated wreck now below as one floats ever upward towards the surface. A thought occurs, maybe the next adventure will be space.

୫⟩━━━━━━━━━━━━━━━━━━━━━━━━━━━━━⟨୧

ABOUT THE AUTHOR

Nolan Soldahl (born April 21, 1995) is married to his wife, Amber Soldahl, whom he met while obtaining his bachelor's degree in Pastoral Studies at Simpson University in Redding, CA. He grew up in the Sacramento valley of California, where he was raised and exposed to many different types and denominations of local churches. He is currently licensed with the Christian & Missionary Alliance and is the Associate Pastor of Missional Ministries at Medford Neighborhood Church in Medford, OR.

nolansoldahl@gmail.com

Cover Photo by Dragos Gontariu on Unsplash

ENDNOTES

1 "Relativism: implies that it is only possible to decide on the truth or falseness of knowledge from within a certain framework and denies the possibility of neutral criteria to decide on the validity of knowledge claims between different frameworks. No objective knowledge exists independent from the knower, so knowledge will be slightly, if not significantly, different in the context of each individual. Usually relativism is assumed to take place in a community through categories of language with narratives."

Berger, Daniel R. Mysterious Romantic Wonder: Engaging Philosophy. 2nd ed. Salem, Ore.: Aretae Publications, 2011. Pg. 217

2 https://www.mmlearn.org/hubfs/docs/OneAnotherPassages.pdf

The "One Another" Passages

The phrase "one another" is derived from the Greek word allelon which means "one another, each other; mutually, reciprocally." It occurs 100 times in the New Testament. Approximately 59 of those occurrences are specific commands teaching us how (and how not) to relate to one another. Obedience to those commands is imperative. It forms the basis for all true Christian community and has a direct impact on our witness to the world (John 13:35). In addition to allelon, the Bible uses other words and phrases to instruct us how to relate to others. With that in mind, the following list is not exhaustive, and primarily focuses on the use of allelon.

POSITIVE COMMANDS

❖ Love one another (John 13:34 - This command occurs at least 16 times)
❖ Be devoted to one another (Romans 12:10)
❖ Honor one another above yourselves (Romans 12:10)
❖ Live in harmony with one another (Romans 12:16)
❖ Build up one another (Romans 14:19; 1 Thessalonians 5:11)
❖ Be likeminded towards one another (Romans 15:5)
❖ Accept one another (Romans 15:7)
❖ Admonish one another (Romans 15:14; Colossians 3:16)
❖ Greet one another (Romans 16:16)
❖ Care for one another (1 Corinthians 12:25)
❖ Serve one another (Galatians 5:13)

- ❖ Bear one another's burdens (Galatians 6:2)
- ❖ Forgive one another (Ephesians 4:2, 32; Colossians 3:13)
- ❖ Be patient with one another (Ephesians 4:2; Colossians 3:13)
- ❖ Speak the truth in love (Ephesians 4:15, 25)
- ❖ Be kind and compassionate to one another (Ephesians 4:32)
- ❖ Speak to one another with psalms, hymns and spiritual songs (Ephesians 5:19)
- ❖ Submit to one another (Ephesians 5:21, 1 Peter 5:5)
- ❖ Consider others better than yourselves (Philippians 2:3)
- ❖ Look to the interests of one another (Philippians 2:4)
- ❖ Bear with one another (Colossians 3:13)
- ❖ Teach one another (Colossians 3:16)
- ❖ Comfort one another (1 Thessalonians 4:18)
- ❖ Encourage one another (1 Thessalonians 5:11)
- ❖ Exhort one another (Hebrews 3:13)
- ❖ Stir up [provoke, stimulate] one another to love and good works (Hebrews 10:24)
- ❖ Show hospitality to one another (1 Peter 4:9)
- ❖ Employ the gifts that God has given us for the benefit of one another (1 Peter 4:10)
- ❖ Clothe yourselves with humility towards one another (1 Peter 5:5)
- ❖ Pray for one another (James 5:16)
- ❖ Confess your faults to one another (James 5:16)

NEGATIVE COMMANDS (how not to treat one another)

- ❖ Do not lie to one another (Colossians 3:9)
- ❖ Stop passing judgment on one another (Romans 14:13)
- ❖ If you keep on biting and devouring each other...you'll be destroyed by each other (Galatians 5:15)
- ❖ Let us not become conceited, provoking and envying each other (Galatians 5:26)
- ❖ Do not slander one another (James 4:11)
- ❖ Don't grumble against each other (James 5:9)

We do all this because we are in a real sense "members of one another" (Romans 12:5; Ephesians 4:25).

3 Chan, Francis. *Letters to the Church.* Colorado Springs, CO: David C. Cook, 2018.

[4]The word "synoptic" means "same view" or "all view". It comes from the root word "syn" meaning "with," "same," or "together". "Optic" refers to eyes and our ability to see. Thus the word, when put together, can be properly transformed to "same view" or "all view." Typically, it is used in two ways. First, as in the case of the Synoptic Gospels [5], to refer to a collection of things that are coherent and/or have much the same opinion (hence "same view). Second, it can be used to express the idea of a summary or "synopsis" that, although short, is also comprehensive (hence "all view"). An example of this form is when someone's work might be called a synoptic examination[2]. (Moggach, Douglas. "Bruno Bauer." Stanford University. Stanford University, 07 Mar. 002. Web. 09 Jan. 2015.)(Routledge, (Firm). Concise Routledge Encyclopedia Of Philosophy. London: Routledge, 2000. eBook Academic Collection (EBSCOhost). Web. 9 Jan. 2015.)

[6] "Objective," by Dwayne H. Mulder The Internet Encyclopedia of Philosophy, ISSN 2161-0002, http://www.iep.utm.edu/objectiv/, 01/22/15.

[7] Routledge Staff (Rudolf A. Makkreel. Concise Routledge Encyclopedia of Philosophy. Florence, KY, USA: Routledge, 2000. ProQuest ebrary. Web. 22 January 2015. Pg. 211

[8] Berger, Daniel R. *Mysterious Romantic Wonder: Engaging Philosophy*. 2nd ed. Salem, Ore.: Aretae Publications, 2011. Pg. 107

[9] Romans 1:20, trans. ESV

[10] "Merriam-Webster Dictionary" Dictionary. Accessed April 17, 2015. http://www.merriam-webster.com/dictionary/opinion

[11]" Relativism: implies that it is only possible to decide on the truth or falseness of knowledge from within a certain framework and denies the possibility of neutral criteria to decide on the validity of knowledge claims between different frameworks. No objective knowledge exists independent from the knower, so knowledge will be slightly, if not significantly, different in the context of each individual. Usually relativism is assumed to take place in a community through categories of language with narratives."
Berger, Daniel R. *Mysterious Romantic Wonder: Engaging Philosophy*. 2nd ed. Salem, Ore.: Aretae Publications, 2011. Pg. 217

[12] Glanzberg, Michael, "Truth", The Stanford Encyclopedia of Philosophy (Fall 2014 Edition), Edward N. Zalta (ed.), URL = <http://plato.stanford.edu/archives/fall2014/entries/truth/>.

[13] "Truth," by Bradley Dowden and Norman Swartz *The Internet Encyclopedia of Philosophy*, ISSN 2161-0002, http://www.iep.utm.edu/truth/#H6, 02/12/15.

[14] John 8:32.NIV

[15] "Objective," by Dwayne H. Mulder *The Internet Encyclopedia of Philosophy*, ISSN 2161-0002, http://www.iep.utm.edu/objectiv/, 01/22/15.

[16] Berger, Daniel R. *Mysterious Romantic Wonder: Engaging Philosophy*. 2nd ed. Salem, Ore.: Aretae Publications, 2011. Pg. 248

[17] "Knowledge," by Stephen Hetherington The Internet Encyclopedia of Philosophy, ISSN 2161-0002, http://www.iep.utm.edu/knowledg/, 02/12/15.

[18] Ichikawa, Jonathan Jenkins and Steup, Matthias, "The Analysis of Knowledge", The Stanford Encyclopedia of Philosophy (Spr 2014 Ed.), Edward N. Zalta (ed.), URL= <http://plato.stanford.edu/archives/spr2014/entries/knowledge-analysis/>.

[19] Hursthouse, Rosalind, "Virtue Ethics", *The Stanford Encyclopedia of Philosophy* (Fall 2013 Edition), Edward N. Zalta (ed.), URL = <http://plato.stanford.edu/archives/fall2013/entries/ethics-virtue/>.
[20] "Virtue," by Nafsika Athanassoulis *The Internet Encyclopedia of Philosophy*, ISSN 2161-0002, http://www.iep.utm.edu/virtue, 02/24/15.

9781732024663